"PORN-AHOLIC"

EXPOSE THE SECRET
AND
SAVE YOUR LIFE

By: Zerek L. Baker Sr.

McClure Publishing, Inc.
Oak Lawn, Illinois

Copyright © 2008
Zerek L. Baker Sr. for McClure Publishing, Inc.

All rights reserved. Printed and bound in the United States of America. No part of this book may be reproduced or utilized in any form or by any means, electronic or mechanical, including photocopying, recording, or by any information storage or retrieval system, except by a reviewer who may quote brief passages in a review to be printed in a magazine or newspaper, without permission in writing from the Publisher: Inquiries should be addressed to McClure Publishing, Inc. Permissions Department, 9624 S. Cicero Avenue, #175, Oak Lawn, Illinois 60453. First Printing: January 8, 2008.

Unless otherwise indicated all scriptural quotations are from the King James Version (KJV) of the Bible. The author and publisher have made every effort to ensure the accuracy and completeness of information contained in this book, we assume no responsibility for errors, inaccuracies, omissions, or any inconsistency therein.

Any slights of people, places, belief systems or organizations are unintentional. Any resemblance to anyone living, dead or somewhere in between is truly coincidental.

ISBN-13	978-0-9790450-3-5
ISBN-10	0-9790450-3-7
LCCN:	20079452552

Cover design by Barron Steward (www.barronsteward.com)
Photograph by Advanced Multimedia Productions, Inc.
(www.ampvideophoto.com)
Interior Layout by Kathy McClure
(www.mcclurepublishing.com)

To order additional copies, please contact.
McClure Publishing, Inc.
www.mcclurepublishing.com
800.659.4908
mcclurepublishing@msn.com

CONTENTS

Page

INTRODUCTION 9

ONE - The Seed of Iniquity 11

TWO - Is the Power Off? 19

THREE - What She Doesn't Know Can Kill Her......27

FOUR - That Shall He Also Reap..........................37

FIVE - Get Fortified For the Battle.........................43

SIX - Pornography and the Single Guy 65

SEVEN - She Loves Me, She Loves Me Not 79

EIGHT - The Sins of the Father.............................83

NINE - Take The Risk 89

TEN - You Deserve the Best 93

ELEVEN - Your Mind; The Battle Field..................99

PRAYER..109

SCRIPTURE REFERENCES 111

BIOGRAPHY 113

DEDICATION

I dedicate this book first and foremost to my Heavenly Father without whom I can do nothing. It is my honor and pleasure to be *used by him* in service to my fellow man, because only God is able to truly restore a life that has been ravaged by pornography addiction.

To my parents Earl & Mary Baker, who instilled in me morals and principals, which in spite of my foolish choices, still served as a foundation of stability that gave strength to my resolve to preserve my marriage, as you have so gracefully for over a half century. The value of your influence on my life is impossible to measure.

To my four older siblings, Paula, Blanche, Fleming and Brigitte, I thank you all for indulging your funny and 'peculiar' little brother and for allowing me to be a little different, as you undoubtedly recognized at some point that I was destined to be. *Many good times lay ahead for us gang.*

To my mother-in-law Bertha Davis (who will probably never speak to me again if she doesn't get a mention in here somewhere.) I love you Mom #2. You totally destroy all the stereotypes about the meddlesome, over-bearing mother-in law. You've always loved me as your own son and never hesitated to let me know it.

(And thanks for always telling your daughter how lucky she is to have me.)

To my two incredible children, Alleece and Zerek Jr. who have become amazing young adults (thanks mostly to a great mom). I pray that my influence in your lives has been positive and beneficial in molding you to fulfill God's purpose for each of you. I also pray that we've developed your strength of character to the point you're able to withstand any undue attention or ill-effects that may potentially arise as a result of my revelations in this book. Just know that you two were reason for the cure and none of the cause.

Finally, to the most important person of all, my gorgeous wife, Patrice Baker. The one with whom I cannot wait to experience the rest of my life. The one who's so awesome, I still have trouble believing God didn't make some slight blunder when he entrusted you to me. The one without whom there would be no book, because had I lost you, I would surely be to devastated to desire to speak, much less put my ramblings to pen and paper. The debt of gratitude I owe you for simply sticking it out through my years of ineptitude, it would take a lifetime to repay. You've always believed in me more than I did myself and I thank and cherish you for having the patience to wait for "that man" to show up. God gave me you to help me become who He made me to be.

A Note to the Wives ...

I saw the shame in his eyes but at that moment it was hard to give a care. I could see his humiliation but pity for him was hard to muster up. The anger, hurt and disgust that overwhelmed me made it very difficult to grant him any compassion. I had the choice to either forgive him or leave. Obviously, I chose to forgive. At some level, I took this as an insult to my competency as a wife and a lover, but I had to quickly dispose of that notion. This was not about me. I discovered that addiction is Satan's attack on one's mind and emotions. So I prayed that God would grant me the grace necessary to forgive my husband in the same manner that he has extended mercy and forgiveness of sin to me.

Zerek's candidness in sharing his problem with pornography, I believe will give insight into how Satan can attack a mind ungoverned by Godly principles. I also believe that Zerek gives the reader nuggets of information on how to diffuse the attack over your mind, gain control over your thought-life and victory for your life.

We have been married for over 24 years and I have personally watched him change from a man whose concept of intimacy was clearly motivated by self-gratification, to a husband who genuinely puts me and my needs above his own.

I love my husband and have great respect for him. He is my very best friend but what stands far above even our close relationship as husband and wife is his genuine love for the Lord. He is a true worshiper of the Lord Jesus Christ.

May God open your eyes in understanding as you and your husband read this book and may the very same grace which He bestowed upon us bring restoration and freedom to your life and marriage.

…but with God all things are possible.
(Matthew 19:26)

            The Wife…

INTRODUCTION

Although I am a Christian and confess Jesus Christ as my Lord and Savior, this book is not written to fellow Christians only. The secret sin of pornography addiction has no cultural, social, religious, racial or economic boundaries. No human being is immune to its seduction or to some related form of fleshly desire born of lust. My personal desire is that everyone would come to know and accept Christ, but my passion and burden is for every person that is in bondage to the psychological prison of secrecy and enslaved by pornography, to be set free. I hate the sin of pornography, but I know that it is far too pervasive in this world's society to ever believe that it can be completely eradicated.

Victory begins with the admission that you're in bondage and the confession to those important to you, that you've lived a life of secret sin. As long as it's kept secret you can never be free of guilt, shame and condemnation. You will always be threatened by the fear of exposure and the risk of public humiliation that will come with discovery.

Trying to wipe out porn is not feasible. That would be like trying to outlaw evil thoughts from all humans. Pornography is a curse in the earth and is a result of the twisted, fallen nature of mankind. Jesus prayed that God would not remove us from the earth, but that He would keep us from the evil in it.

I believe it is possible that God's healing power could totally remove the desire for pornographic self-stimulation. However, I don't believe that this is most men's experience. I believe that most men, even those who profess to follow Christ, have to battle against the lust of the flesh on a daily basis.

My assignment is to reach as many individuals as my God has pre-destined for me to reach and to encourage them towards the defeat of this life-corroding addiction in which I found myself for many, many years.

CHAPTER 1 – **THE SEED OF INIQUITY**

So there we were, three innocent little boys playing in the alley as many inner city youths did in the late sixties on the west side of Chicago. Just minding our own business doing what little boys do in alleys: play baseball, basketball, throw rocks, ride bikes, etc.

Then one of us noticed a magazine sticking out of a garbage can. On the pages of that magazine was something I had never seen before but would be profoundly affected by: totally naked human flesh in full color, high gloss, awe-inspiring luminescence. I cannot remember the name of the magazine but I can still recall the impact of the images and all of our reactions to it. We ran immediately to a place of secrecy; a vacant partially constructed house in the middle of the block where we excitedly scanned every page in wide-eyed amazement.

After sometime, we stashed the magazine in what we thought to be a safe place. I can remember the trio of us venturing back for more on several occasions that day and sometimes bringing along a friend or two, to share our big discovery with.

I remember being unable to forget those pictures all evening and I could hardly wait till the next day to get back to that hiding place, only to find the magazine gone. One of those scoundrels had made off with the goods.

It's funny, but even then I can recall not being able to accuse anyone else of taking the magazine or being upset at the other guys because deep down inside I knew that I was doing something wrong by just looking at it and getting such a thrill from it. *The beginning of unrighteousness.* The seed was planted and the enemy waited for more opportunities to water and tend to that seed.

One such opportunity came several years later when I discovered a pornographic magazine in my older brother's bedroom. Don't ask me how I happened to be in his room *"discovering"* a magazine underneath his mattress. I honestly don't remember, but I was probably snooping in typical "annoying-little- brother" fashion.

Anyway, this event accelerated my slide into the porno cesspool in a major way because these books depicted females and males in the literal act of sexual relations. This image is generally only imagined by young boys or perhaps shown in some hygiene textbook in a totally sanitized and elementary version, for educational purposes only. Now there was nothing left to the imagination and for a boy entering puberty, you could not pick a better season to plant a poisonous time-bomb such as this; a twisted and thorny shrub that's practically guaranteed to bloom in very aggressive fashion in the future. These roots will stretch deep into the soul and become embedded in areas of his sub-conscious that may not be uncovered for years, if at all.

I now had a readily accessible supply of stimuli for my growing porn habit. For a horny teenaged boy this is equivalent to a young fashion "Diva" discovering that she has after hour access to Nordstrom's shoe department and the codes to disarm the security system….. **Heaven**!!

One of the subtle dangers of pornography is that, on its surface it appears to be a totally harmless habit. No one's involved except you, your magazine of choice and "Mr. Johnson." But as I mentioned before, this poison is aggressive. At a point it will begin to need more powerful images to achieve the same level of stimulation, and like most addictions, it also has a devastating "time-sapping" component to it, which we'll talk more about in later chapters.

Following this *"discovery"* episode, there weren't really any significant events to speak of in regard to this habit during my teenage years. I was a walking contradiction of sorts. I was a musician who never did drugs, never smoked, never got drunk or even drank beer; I was a somewhat talented athlete who didn't chase skirts; I had many friends, but a boring social life; I lusted after girls that I never had the guts to talk to. So girlfriends were few, although my relationships were long by high school standards. Pornography served as the stereotypical *release* for the sex life I wasn't having but that all my peers believed we were supposed to have.

I do recall during those years though, the introduction of cable television into our household. Watching late one night, purely by accident while flipping channels, I noticed that when passing by the adult programming (which we did not subscribe to), for a brief second the picture would flash before the channel scrambler distorted the screen. Of course this peaked the meter of my highly sensitive porno-detector. With a little patience and twisted determination I found that if I flipped back and forth just fast enough, I could sustain enough of the picture to make out certain figures and actions on the program. Not quite "Heaven," but enough to feed the beast some new stimuli. These were *real people* in the act of having *real sex*. I had glimpsed the next frontier: X-rated movies.

I remember waiting patiently each night for everyone to go to bed and I'd stealthily make my way to the TV for my nightly dosage. It's quite astounding how skillful one can become with the "clicker." If anyone came in the room unexpectantly, I could change that channel and adjust the volume faster than Wyatt Earp could draw down in a gunfight. Fathers, keep a watchful eye on your young men during late night TV. In fact, I would advise you to ban late night TV all together.

I awaited my 21st birthday with great anticipation. Not because I was legally becoming a man in the eyes of society, but because I could now legally enter an adult movie theatre. You see, once the new concept of movies was introduced to my sub-conscious mind, I suddenly began to notice all of the X-rated movie advertisements in the weekend newspaper. A new and improved and more potent visual format had been introduced. Deeper went the poisonous roots into my soul and greater grew the need for a more intense level of eroticism. Pornography does not seek simply to invade, it seeks to conquer and destroy.

So not long after the big 2-1, I ventured into my first adult movie theatre. Right away my first impulse, if I had been in my right mind of course, would have been to turn around and stroll right back outta' there because the smell in this place I knew was not quite normal. It reeked of something I had never encountered before but I knew it was human in origin. It had the stench of unclean flesh with a hint of urine or some other bodily secretion. (*Whatever you're imagining right now is probably correct*). Regardless of the odor, my lust drove me onward. As I entered the theatre the 20-foot large, fully nude, real-life sexual intercourse taking place on the screen immediately assaulted my brain. I will not go into further detail because if you're reading this book odds are you've seen much of the same things I have. I also know that for an addict, too much detail can be a trigger much like an ex-smoker or an ex-alcoholic venturing back into the bar scene. All it takes is a whiff or in our case a suggestion that brings to mind sexual images which can stimulate the senses and lead to spontaneous arousal.

Needless to say, I would never be the same. It is truly astonishing to think about how the gift of physical intimacy and God ordained human intercourse has been so twisted and perverted in this earthly realm. Sexual desire is perfectly natural and the power of the sexual urge can be observed throughout all of nature, particularly in the male species. The command to "be fruitful, multiply and replenish the earth," as it pertains to human kind, would be impossible without it. However, unlike animals or other creeping, flying or swimming things, human sex drive is not purely instinctive. It can be willfully directed or controlled. It can be released not just for procreation but also for simple self-gratification. It can be used to express genuine love and the giving of oneself to another in the most intimate of ways; or it can be used as a tool of abuse, denial of affection or lustful debauchery. Totally wicked abominations such as pedophilia, rape, bestiality, incest, sodomy, sado-masochism and homosexuality have been fused into the human psyche and even adopted as acceptable sexual practices by some groups.

Pornography in its mildest form is but an entry-way into a downward sloping pit. Its attack on the public consciousness is masterfully subtle.

When I scanned that magazine as a young boy, it was in stunned amazement, because in those days the female anatomy could only be imagined and snickered about in full red-faced blush. Those hallowed body parts were simply not to be seen outside of marriage as far as we knew. But just look at the television or print media today. Our minds are flooded with titillating images of women and men in purposely-sensual depictions. "Sex sells" is a common advertising cliché. From lingerie ads, to car commercials, to music videos, the sexually super-charged images continually get more and more provocative.

The poisonous harvest from this seed of wickedness is a nation and a society that is infected with a cancerous growth; a tumor that feeds on its own flesh, until there is nothing left to devour and then it dies. To stop its progression will not be easy, but we must dare to take up the fight. My goal is to lead damaged hearts down the path toward healing and restoration. In regard to the affliction of pornography, my belief is that disarming the stronghold of secrecy is the key to victory and a rejuvenated life.

CHAPTER 2 – IS THE POWER OFF?

Without faith it is impossible to please God. Without righteousness, it is impossible to have faith for anything of significance or that is beyond ordinary. Without a clear conscience and a pure heart it is impossible to have a true sense of righteousness. For instance; if you practice unethical business dealings, it is quite unlikely that you have sincere faith in the power and spiritual connection promised through your tithe, if you're compelled to even tithe at all. If your heart is polluted with guilty secrets, lies and unfaithfulness, you are undoubtedly burdened with condemnation. When you feel condemned you cannot possibly stand before a Holy God; an omnipotent, all-knowing and all seeing Lord and think that you have somehow fooled him.

As a child did you ever experience a situation where you willfully deceived or disobeyed your parent, teacher, coach or anyone you looked-up to and wanted badly to please? Do you remember the look of hurt, shame or disappointment in their eyes? The look that said "why," or "how could you do this to me?" "The one who cares for you, who supports you, who cheers for you, who sacrifices endlessly for you, who gives to you, and who loves you unconditionally. You cannot possibly love me or appreciate me and do what you've done."

That look of disappointment on their face had such powerful impact on you that you couldn't even look them in the eyes, because when you did the depth of their pain could be felt enough to fill you with tears and self-disgust. As a small child you didn't know what to call that feeling or how to process it. You only knew that no *spanking* was necessary. The pain of "the look," left enough of an impact to know that you never wanted to see it again or to do anything that would bring it back.

That's much the way you feel as an adult coming before God with a sense of unrighteousness or guilt consciousness. You would rather hide than face him. You'd rather continue the charade, displaying "a form of godliness, but denying the power thereof."

Imagine an apple or any piece of fruit being plucked from the vine. For many hours, even days, the fruit will still appear to be alive and flourishing just as it did on the tree. But in reality that fruit died the moment it became separated from its life-sustaining source. That fruit no longer has the ability to grow or to even exist without the connection to its life-giving source. A slow and decaying death is all it has to look forward to. This is also the same fate that awaits those of us who practice a life of secret sin. Because of unrighteousness our connection to our life-giving source (God) is severed, therefore, all true growth ceases and our access to the limitless power of His kingdom is cut off. The pathway to true wisdom and spiritual insight is closed so you will continually battle with the consequences of bad decisions and unsound judgment. You will experience confusion and lack of vision for the future because your only source of trust will be yourself and "a double-minded man is unstable in all his ways." (James 1:8) You'll be filled with self-doubt because you know how untrustworthy you are.

You will lack peace and serenity in your home because through your secret sin you've allowed an open door for other demonic forces to get in, such as strife, rebellion, sexual or marital tension, adultery, financial lack and so on.

When your spirit man is condemned, you will struggle to bear the position of headship in your home. A human being was designed to be an amazingly balanced creature. The spirit, soul (*mind, will, and emotions*) and the body are tuned to operate in perfect harmony. If either of these components are deficient or have been corrupted, then there will be an imbalance in your state of well-being. It is not possible for you to lie to your spouse regarding your whereabouts or your sexual fidelity and still be at total peace within your heart. (If you can, you are what's known as a sociopath and you will require a higher degree of treatment than this book.) But let me be a bit more direct. You are buying that pornography somewhere; a video store, an adult bookstore, online, etc., and you are spending money that you cannot truthfully give an account for; and you are then indulging in the porn either by masturbation or some other form of self-stimulation. If this activity is unbeknownst to your spouse then it's because she thinks you're in one place doing one thing, while you're actually in another place and doing something else.

Trying to maintain this behavior while keeping it a secret is going to cause an imbalance in your inner being. Your soul has been invaded and has overtaken your body. These spiritual parasites have attached themselves and like pirates they're attempting to steer you on a course of destruction.

Your mind is trying to justify, rationalize and compartmentalize the actions of your body, but your spirit is having none of it. Your spirit is that channel or conduit that yearns to be re-connected with God, the source of truth and goodness. Although you may have convinced yourself that everything is "okay" because you seem to be getting away with it, you are in conflict within yourself and the inner turmoil will eventually begin to short-circuit your ability to function in certain capacities.

For example; in order for you to effectively lie to your spouse, you will have to de-sensitize yourself in some fashion because your conscience and sense of right and wrong will not allow you to blatantly hurt someone that you love. Over time, the "de-sensitivity" will become "indifference." When indifference sets up in a relationship, it gives off an energy that says, "I really don't care what you do or say, because I've numbed myself to you, to the degree that my emotions cannot truly be affected by you." When this occurs your offerings or gestures of affection basically become robotic. You're going through the motions but your mate will instinctively pick up a sense that she is not really reaching you or receiving from you at a deeply heartfelt, sincere emotional level. And she'll be correct. This is where we get the saying "the wife always knows." Women have a keen, innate sensitivity for this depth of emotion and they know when there's a fuse blown somewhere in the circuit board because they're not getting the full current.

So now your marital relationship is beginning to become tense which will affect the entire household. These energy and emotion sapping issues will only increase because this poison seed you've planted will grow and spread into more areas of your personality. Indifference will become a characteristic of the way you approach more and more of your life's issues. Motivation and zeal toward betterment in life whether in business, personal relationships, ministry, careers or any endeavor are heavily reliant on passion and desire.

Prolonged indifference will eventually nullify all true passion, which will lead to depression, cynicism and an overall negative view of life and the future.

I floated through years of my life being tossed like a leaf in the wind with no direction and no clear vision for my family's future or for myself. It was only either by God's grace or my own lack of initiative and drive that I was a stable employee and held down jobs for long periods of time. This was good for my family but these jobs were just that; *jobs*. I was shamefully content to toil away at the millstone of someone else's empire while never seeking to have anything substantial of my own. I shied away from anything that was the least bit risky, or that required me to apply myself or move too far out of my comfort zone. I had shown signs of skill and leadership ability that had my supervisors wanting to promote me into positions of higher responsibility, but I would always somehow find a reason to refuse it. It was as if someone had flipped a switch in my sub-conscious and all of a sudden, I would become dissatisfied or unhappy with the job and my productivity would begin to suffer accordingly.

You cannot lie to your inner-self. No matter how impressive or attractive a facade you paint on the outside, deep inside that sense of unrighteousness will begin to erode your self-esteem. You will sub-consciously sabotage your own progress because you don't really feel worthy of a high degree of respect. So you'll lose out on one opportunity after another for advancement but it will appear to have perfectly logical explanations or reasons why it didn't work out for you. Sadly, what's most tragic is that you won't even be moved by the occurrence because your emotions have been so anesthetized by the attitude of indifference.

We will address how to begin to reverse this thought process a bit later, but you can now probably start to see symptoms like these within yourself. If you closely examine your past and present, you can see how this inner-conflict has manifested these types of attitudes concerning many areas of your life. How do you relate to your children? When you're obsessing for some "alone time" to indulge your addiction, what kinds of reasons do you come up with to get rid of them or for not spending that time with them?

If you really want to see a pitiful snapshot of your life, just think about how much of this amazing human experience is going on all around you and around the world. The people most important to you are left to carry on without you. Precious moments stream by without your total involvement and most caring and sincere attentiveness. That exhilaration and heart-pounding excitement that you once felt for your spouse during your courtship is not dead, it's just been depressed by life's issues and replaced with a very poor substitute. The feeling of love and overwhelming wonderment of life that you felt at the birth of your children is not irretrievable but hard work is required to excavate it from underneath years of de-sensitizing waste.

Maybe the zeal you had at your newly found faith seems like a distant memory but it can be restored once you realize that God has not written you off or given up on you.

You must make the decision to reverse this damage starting right now by refusing to accept the notion that you are powerless to overcome this weakness. If you don't, a future littered with pain and regret is inevitable.

CHAPTER 3 – WHAT SHE DOESN'T KNOW, CAN KILL HER

As a married man with two children it is probably noticeable by now that my perspective seems to slant in the direction of men with spouses and the effects of pornography addiction on family relationships. It is obvious that the dynamics would be quite different between men with a spouse versus a man living a single life. I will spend some time highlighting some of the differences and similarities between both scenarios but my main objective in these first chapters is to help you locate yourself. In talking with most men, I find that the snares and enticements that draw a person into this dark life are fairly common to all of us.

The odds are that you've already recognized some familiar situations amongst those that I've described thus far. The introduction; where an emotional or shocking event forms an indelible impression in your mind, i.e., a child viewing live sexual intercourse for the first time. The escalation; where habitual meditation of sexual imagery promotes an increasing appetite for more. Finally, the rationalization and acceptance phase; where you start to totally lose all resistance or any conscience regarding your inappropriate behavior.

There are, however, some profound differences between the ramifications of porn addiction in the life of a married man and that of a single man.

I'd like now to focus on the married man. A treasure that is arguably the easiest and fastest to lose, and is yet the hardest and most time demanding to earn in a marital relationship is the gift of trust. What can take years of consistency, faithfulness, dependability and loyalty to build can be totally destroyed in an afternoon, a moment or an event. I believe that it's no coincidence that the words "Trust" and "Truth" are so similar. All trust must be anchored by truth. This is why a life of secrecy when uncovered is so devastating to the injured spouse.

A woman has a natural desire to feel a sense of security and assurance within her marriage. Although aggressive societal "isms" such as feminism and lesbianism have attempted to undo this natural instinct it still flourishes and holds its place within the organism of the family structure.

In the early years of my marriage like many newly or recently wed couples we had more than our share of problems. United in our very early twenties we were both so inexperienced in so many things, it was only to be expected that we would have a few issues to overcome.

However, I came into it with some unexpected baggage that not even I was aware I had. I had a perfectly modeled example of married life to follow in my parents, whom at this writing are nearing 60 years of blessed union. Not all candy and roses I'm sure but there were no separations or talk of divorce to my knowledge, in the midst of raising five children. So if nothing else, I seem to have picked-up the longevity part of it as my wife and I are in our 24th year together. But something snuck in under the radar with me and in hindsight, I can see how I never would have detected it in a million years.

    I don't recall being very active in pornography at all in those years, but the root was there and it was being nourished by some of its companions, namely lust and lasciviousness or the lack of restraint and self control.

    When we married my wife and I had dated for about a year and a few months. Then came a crises point where her living situation changed and she had to get an apartment on her own. Understand now, we weren't saved or even attending a church at that time. I had been raised in the Baptist faith and my wife had been brought up in the Muslim faith for a time. She no longer professed that religion or any at all when we got together. So being head over heels in love and not able to bear the thought of her living somewhere alone I did the only logical thing a man could do. We shacked-up. Obviously not the morally upright thing to do, but it felt right so who cares, right? I mean everybody's doing it ya'know. Well we did it.

    "It was the best of times.... It was the worst of times."

It was a true learning experience. I learned that an angry woman can part her lips and cut you in ways that would make any samurai warrior jealous; I learned that a man should not kick open a bedroom door in anger, unless he's certain that his girlfriend's face is not 5 inches from the other side; I learned that no matter how good your intentions, thinking you can support a household on about $7.50 an hour is just plain dumb; I also learned that a very petite woman can kick a much larger man down the stairs without much effort if she applies her foot to his back at just the right moment ... (selah).

Then there were the bad times.... No, but seriously, I knew that shacking-up would only be temporary because I had every intention of marrying this woman. When she let go of the chokehold and the color returned to my face, I said "Okay, pick a date!" So after about 16 months or so of living together, we got hitched, fo'real.

I would say we had the typical issues that any newlywed couple would have to overcome; learning to blend two different personalities into one. However, as I look back now, I believe the secrecy factor was evident in small ways even then. The unbridled lust for fleshly, erotic stimulation creates an open pathway into your soul through your imagination. It is said that whatever you meditate or consistently focus your imagination upon, you will draw towards yourself.

Men who allow themselves the freedom to have a "roving eye" are unaware of the traps they are potentially setting for themselves. That roving eye will eventually make contact with another set of eyes that will return the glance and set in motion a chain of events that will only lead to great pain and heartbreak.

I also had such an eye when we married and in our sixth year of marriage, I was enticed into a brief but no less adulterous office romance with a female co-worker. Even after almost twenty years the sting of the shame, regret and embarrassment of my unfaithfulness is strong enough to bring on extreme condemnation. Not to mention re-living the pain that this caused my wife, and how I foolishly jeopardized everything that I consider most precious, my family. Once you get comfortable with harboring secrets there is practically no limit to the things you can lie about and learn to live with.

My adultery was facilitated by a lack of moral boundaries or self-restraint, a.k.a. lasciviousness. This is a direct result of a seared conscience; a conscience that is numb and driven mostly by a need to please self and cares little about the feelings of others. As mentioned earlier, this characteristic is associated with that spirit of indifference, that's needed to bolster the capacity to lie with callousness.

It was purely by the Grace of God that our marriage survived. It took many years to regain my wife's trust and acceptance. I did whatever I had to do to re-assure her that I could again be trusted but once trust has been broken, the fracture may heal, however, the scar of unfaithfulness will remain. There will be a scab of suspicion over her heart designed to protect it from ever being hurt the same way again.

The purity and sanctity of complete trust is akin to that of virginity. Once violated, it can never be restored to its original state of purity. The process of rebuilding trust in a marriage is much the same as mending a relationship that's been defiled by pornography addiction. After the secret violation has been revealed, you must now find some method of re-establishing accountability. You will have to prove on a regular basis that you are committed to correcting whatever vices you're dealing with.

The secret of my addiction wasn't discovered until many years later when my wife came across a video that I had stashed away somewhere. (What you do in the dark will eventually come to light). Even though it was every bit as embarrassing, horrifying and humiliating as I feared it would be; in having my secret exposed, there was yet an unexplainable sense of relief.

Though I truly believed I was very close to losing my wife and family, at least I didn't have the burden of trying to hide this hideous weakness any longer. It was very much like the liberation I feel now in writing this book and making the decision to help others to attack this perversity head-on.

I believe also that it was only because of that protective scab on my wife's heart from my first infraction that she was able to hold out through the second. She knew that she could never again with any certainty say what her husband wouldn't do. She had to always consider it a real possibility that I could again lie to her about a recurrence of either of these sinful acts or perhaps worse.

My punishment and eternal regret is in the knowledge that I am the one who destroyed that pure bond of trust in my marriage and that I will never be able to remove that blemish from her memory.

Those violations of her trust also diminished her capacity to respect and honor me as her husband and as the head of the family. The weakening of trust equates to uncertainty about her future and causes major doubt within her as to whether or not she can depend on me to come through for her or to even be around in the future.

If she cannot trust that I'm totally committed to her and to our success as a marriage, how can she totally trust me to make the right decisions for the family? She will consciously or subconsciously begin to scrutinize my actions and analyze my direction, filtering everything through her highly sensitive, protective maternal instincts.

If your spouse receives any impulses that you're not "all there" and totally on the mark in your choices, she will have uneasiness in her spirit and after all she's been through with you, she will not refrain from letting you know of her disagreement with your ideas or course of action. She'll say in so many words "because I cannot totally trust you, I cannot totally rest my future and my children's futures in your unpredictable and untrustworthy hands." This is a tragically sad and hurtful place for a marriage to be, please take my word for it.

A man has a built in need to be respected and honored by his wife. Without it he cannot righteously assume his position as head of household because her willful submission to his authority empowers him in his role. She is not inherently subservient to him. It is not possible to submit to someone unless you at least had <u>equal</u> authority to begin with. By her submission she is saying, "I don't <u>have</u> to, but because I love and trust you, I will decide to submit my own authority to your vision and leadership."

All of that goes out-the-window when secrets are kept, then exposed, and trust is squandered. An existence such as this will drain years from your life; years that are being stolen from you and by default, from your wife because she has hitched her wagon to you, her stallion. Whatever potential for a brilliant and happy future that was evident from the beginning, has been sapped from you like helium from a pinpricked balloon.

You do not have to continue down this road to devastation if you don't wish to. When you consider the negative impact on the life of this amazing creature that God entrusted to you and place the proper value on her; the will to change should be passionately ignited within you. You do have the ability to overcome addiction to pornography just as with any other form of addiction or habitual substance abuse.

The ability lies within the infinite power of your mind to impress it's will upon your flesh, as it is empowered by the spiritual connection to the true source of all power; God.

The male gender has been under attack since the Garden of Eden. Men are not only the foundation of the Family; it was God's intent that the foundation for all of human society would rest upon the shoulders of the man. Because our mortal enemy knew that he could never fulfill his ultimate desire to destroy all humankind, he set out to do the next best thing and seduce us into destroying ourselves.

So now in addition to suffering such naturally destructive forces as plagues, pestilence, wildfires, famines and weather related disasters; we also contend with unseen attacks from within. Compelled by invisible pressures and environmental stimulus, we can be sub-consciously programmed to act against our own best interests as a species and hatefully influenced to commit unspeakable suffering upon ourselves such as through genocide or terrorism.

    Our enemy knows that the human mind is the doorway through which we are most vulnerable. Until we realize this and become vigilant in protecting our environments from negative and debasing input we will continue to lose in the battle to uphold decency and morality in our society.

CHAPTER 4 — THAT SHALL HE ALSO REAP

As it pertains to human life, destruction can come in many forms. To trace back to the root causes of many of our personal trials may call for more introspection than the average person will want to take time and energy to do. It can also be a painful exercise to take on.

There are cause and effect principles in operation throughout our entire lives and much of what we experience as hardships and trials (the effects) you may never be able to trace back to a direct action or a clearly visible reason for it, (the cause).

The title line for this chapter was derived from a scripture that actually reads, "Be ye not deceived, God is not mocked; for whatsoever a man soweth, that shall he also reap." (Galatians 6:7) If I were a farmer this concept would be easily understandable because I'd be operating from the positive benefits of the principle. To "sow" means to plant, to "reap" means to harvest or to get back a return. If I plant corn seeds, I will reap corn crops. If I plant tomato seeds I am going to get a harvest of tomatoes after the seeds have reached maturity.

There is another scripture associated with this principle that is relevant specifically for mankind that reads; "If you sow (plant) to the flesh, you shall reap (harvest) corruption (or destruction)." (Galatians 6:8 para.) This principle or universal law clearly tells me that when I sow time and indulgence into fleshly gratifying behaviors such as lust, fornication, adultery or pornography I can expect to reap destruction as an end result. The problem with destruction or corruption is that they are broad terms that cannot easily be defined in this context.

Pornography addiction is a sickness of the mind. Our minds are fed through our five major senses; hearing, sight, touch, taste and smell. Through these 5 receptors information is fed into our conscious and subconscious mind which comprises our imagination. God's word tells us that the human imagination is so powerful a force that when it is focused with singleness of purpose, it cannot be restrained from achieving its objective. (Genesis 11:6)

Our enemy is all too aware of this power within us. Because he has the power to effect this earthly environment, he uses the forces subject to him to manipulate circumstances and apply pressure or suggestive influences that we perceive through our senses. The images we see and the communications we hear form the dominant impressions in our minds that we see as life experiences. These experiences all come together to make up our belief systems, our comprehension of right and wrong or good and evil and the scope of our hopes and desires. We also refer to this as our moral values and principles.

In comparison with all the other ills facing humanity, pornography would appear pretty insignificant and trivial. I mean, if a guy or gal wants to hunker-down with a weeks worth of "skin-flicks" and self stimulate til' their eyes bug out, who's it really affecting, right? As long as they're in the privacy of their own place, right? There in lies the wicked, subtle genius of Satan's plan.

In the early days of what's now the Gay Rights movement, the cry of the homosexuals was "what do you care what we do behind closed doors, it's none of your business." A couple of decades later it was "don't ask, don't tell" as they demanded their acceptance into the military. Today we cannot mention God or Jesus in a public school but you can be jailed and charged with promoting hate crimes for simply speaking out too loudly against the teaching of "same-sex" or "trans-gendered" lifestyles in those same public schools.

There used to be a negative stigma attached to the sin of pornography. In essence there still is, otherwise why would so many men be enslaved by the secrecy of its indulgence? I believe it's because at man's core is a connection to a divine source, a Creator. In my faith He is called Jehovah, the one true living God. Other faiths have other names for it. But most people when asked will acknowledge some being higher than themselves, which has providence over man's affairs.

My God commands that 'thou shalt have no other Gods before me." (Exodus 20:3) Directing your worship towards any other object we classify as "idolatry" or the worship of a false God. Our mortal enemy sought to esteem himself higher than God. He is the originator of self-love, or self-worship. To love yourself or to lift up your own lustful desires above everyone and everything else is a character trait that descends from this lineage. Homosexuality is a manifestation of the ultimate result of self-love. The prefix "Homo" means *same*. Practitioners of homosexuality focus as the object of their desires on the "same sex" or "same gender" within their own species. Homosexual, therefore means *same sex* or *one sex*. The term *same* when applied to an individual can be interpreted "one just like *myself*." Any distortion of the significance or esteem of oneself can lead to or be characterized as "self-ish." The suffix "ish" can be translated "nature" or "resembling." Homosexual as it relates to selfishness then means: to love or exalt one with the same nature as; or who resembles myself. The defining characteristic of the male gender is their sex organ called the penis. The term penis originates from the Greek word "phallus" which means a symbol for or representation of the male sexual organ.

Certain ancient civilizations worshiped false gods of fertility and fashioned large statues to which they performed rituals of worship. These distorted religions made idols of the male organ and formed the genesis for what became homosexuality. A deeper study of the religious practices in the days of Nimrod will bear this out.

Pornography is therefore an extension of this type of idol worship. It causes you to place your own sexual fulfillment above all else. By indulging in idolatry you are violating one of God's laws and this again leads to a sense of unrighteousness and alienation from God.

If great numbers of men both in and out of the church are spiritually and sub-consciously weakened by this addiction and in bondage to guilty secrets, is there any wonder why the moral values and principles of our society are being eroded as we stand and watch with our eyes wide shut.

Our men, the foundation of our society have been rendered totally ineffective and powerless by our own hands. Our legal system is being circumvented and laws that served to establish our nation as a standard for the entire world and a beacon of hope are being re-written by those who desire a lower standard or a type of relativism. One might not count this to be a symptom of porn because it is quite difficult to connect pornography with a societal breakdown caused by the weakening of the critical male role in its structure. That's precisely what makes it such a devious and effective tool. When the male psyche has been so warped and demoralized over decades by the slow corrosion of our cherished traditional values, history has shown that the fall of an entire nation can be the result.

CHAPTER 5 — **GET FORTIFIED FOR THE BATTLE**

I would like to state clearly for the record that I write this book not as an authority on this subject or to in anyway imply that I'm able to sit in judgment of men who for whatever reason do not feel led to take the same steps of "self-outing" as I have. I was compelled to do this and I have received it as a calling on my life, to address a human affliction or vice with which I have had many years of painful personal experience. As a result of those experiences and my journey through them, I have formulated what I believe to be a practical and realistic set of disciplines that may not work for everyone, but that have given me a degree of victory over this problem. I use the phrase "degree of victory" because I recognize that as long as there are very active, very real forces of temptation, that are totally committed to my destruction, I can never relax and let down my guard if I am to maintain my stance against this enemy.

The Apostle Paul wrote that he must "die daily to the flesh" in regard to bringing his fleshly desires under submission. He also wrote of a "thorn in the flesh" which he repeatedly begged of the Lord to take or remove from him. There is some debate about just what this "thorn" was, however, this was a man who received 39 lashes 5 times; was beaten with rods 3 times; stoned once; shipwrecked 3 times; imprisoned, exiled, scorned and much more. For him to have had the anointing and the grace of God to survive all that, you have to ask yourself, what of mere <u>flesh</u> could he not overcome? Furthermore, if there was something he couldn't whip, what chance does a '*couch- potato*' like me have, who can barely make it through a 24 hour fast.

The fact that he had to mentally and spiritually constrain his flesh daily, speaks volumes to the internal struggle we face and the tremendous force of the pressure that can be brought against the governors of our behavioral will. The book of Jeremiah states "the heart is deceitful above all things and desperately wicked; who can know it?" (Jeremiah 17:9)

Because we tend to do things that are totally contrary to our own best interests, we must enforce strict discipline over our habits and employ the use of practical safeguards for ourselves. Reinforcement is needed to uphold the decisions we make in regards to our conduct and even more importantly, to constrain our thought-lives. If you decide to live morally upright and set high standards of decency and modesty within a society that is growing increasingly more decadent, understand that your senses are going to be relentlessly bombarded with images of sensuality.

It has been my experience that there is not one technique or tool that will do the trick in every instance. The same thing that squelched your urges last month may not do as good a job this month.

The enemy will figure out your (m.o.) and he'll apply a different strategy for the next assault. The key is to recognize that he really only has a limited arsenal and you have the ability to spot his devices and diffuse them before they get close to penetrating your defenses.

One pretty effective tool he used on me for many years was the "sexually dissatisfied husband" rationale. He will take any convenient set of circumstances such as pregnancy, your spouse's temporary but lingering illness, menstrual cycles, her fatigue due to her job, or any combination of these and others. You string a couple of them back-to-back and pretty soon it's feeling like a *long* time since you've seen any action. Well you're not gonna be an immoral, unfaithful louse and go sneakin' around with some home-wrecker and jeopardize your marriage. But a man's gotta do *somethin'*, right? I mean, you sympathize with her and everything, but hey, *you got needs Bro!* And right about now those needs are talkin' at you pretty loud. What's a man supposed to do? ...*and the trap is set*.

So you make it "Okay" within yourself to use alternative methods to ease your pain. "It's not like I'm hurting anybody" you'll tell yourself. There is probably not a husband alive who has not felt this way at some point in time and I can tell you that the pressure you're feeling is real. You do have needs. In general, men have more of a natural need for sex than women because for men sex is a form of release and not a function of emotion. Sex is more fulfilling and much more passionate when there is a romantic or loving emotional connection, but a man does not require those elements to be sexually satisfied and can still reach a climax quite effectively without them.

I found this to be a great starting point to begin to chip away at the enemy's stronghold on my life. You see at some point you've got to acknowledge and accept the fact that you have a weakness. That weakness is your inability to override the commands of your flesh. You must begin to see a literal separation between you and your flesh, because in actuality they are two totally different entities.

Let me state again for the record that I am not a psychologist or a mental health expert, but neither are most of the men and women dealing with these issues so my explanations on this subject will be directed to them from an "average Joe's" perspective at the best of my ability to break it down. The human physiology is more complex than man himself will ever come close to fully comprehending because we were created by a God that is infinitely more intelligent than our limited imaginations can even begin to grasp without supernatural revelation knowledge from Him.

I know that was a mouthful and my apologies to any unbelievers who may read this, but I had to get that out. (Aaahhhh....) Okay, here goes.

I will refer to these two entities as the (conscious will) and the (subconscious will). Your conscious will is what you think to do, and then proceed to go ahead and do. Your sub-conscious will is what you might consciously tell yourself you want to do but you go ahead and proceed to do the exact opposite, or vice-versa. For instance; you tell yourself today, out loud, that you are going to start a diet or a fast tomorrow. You then go to bed that night. You awake the next morning. You go through your usual routine but you haven't forgotten that you said you're going to start that diet today. You get in the car, start driving, the next thing you know you've pulled into the Duncan Donuts drive-thru just like you've done everyday for the last "umpteen" weeks. Now you've got half a double-chocolate donut devoured before it clicks; "Oh, no!" … "Oh well, I guess I'll start that diet tomorrow."

You have just fallen victim to the programming of your sub-conscious will. This part of your mind has the power to override decisions that you have made consciously. This works in the positive as well as the negative.

I must also factor into this equation a third and most important component which is the *spirit* man. Your spirit is the *real you* and it is ultimately more powerful than your conscious or sub-conscious will. I guess I would more accurately describe it as a "driver" of your conscious or sub-conscious will.

To effectively engage in the battle for control of your flesh it is essential that you gain at least a basic understanding of the controllers that trigger your impulses and actions. I characterize your spirit as the actual life force within you. Have you ever wondered what it is that keeps a human heart beating? Just about anything in our earthly environment that's been created by man and has mechanical motion requires a power source such as a battery or electricity. What source keeps us ticking? I believe that source to be our spirit and that it is connected to the highest source of power and wisdom and understanding which is God.

Although the spirit is the most powerful component of our being, it will not supersede your conscious and sub-conscious will without your authorization and submission. You will eventually need to enlist help for your conscious will, because the pornography root is buried deep within your subconscious mind from years of programming via your habitual practices. You will find that it takes more than just telling yourself you won't do it anymore to re-program your mind. It's going to take something powerful enough to 're-create' your entire self-image and mental paradigm. For a Christian, this process begins through the acceptance of Jesus Christ as our Lord and Savior, which enables us, by Faith, to be spiritually re-born into a new life and empowered by a new system of belief.

For a non-believer it will likely require a traumatic event or some shocking and emotionally trying moment or period in your life such as a divorce, a life-threatening incident or the death of a loved one. Something that will cause you to want to totally erase your past and transform yourself into a completely new you. A word to the wise; try Jesus first. It's a lot simpler and if it doesn't work for you, you've got all the rest of your life to try pain, anguish, and fear of death, trauma or divorce, right? Surely one of those is a cinch to "git'er done" for ya'.

Back to my point, I found that I first began to realize that I could arrest some control back from my flesh when I discovered my first strategy through the use of fasting.

Get A Victory Over the Flesh

I had heard about the power of fasting and prayer for years but I never actually believed in it because truthfully, I could never get beyond about 36 hours without having to shove something down my gullet. As soon as I caved in on that part of it the enemy had me so defeated and disappointed with myself that I felt too condemned to pray with any real conviction. And during those 36 hours he slammed me so constantly with thoughts of food that I couldn't even focus on anything else anyway so I never really got in any effective prayer time throughout the whole ordeal.

Then one day my wife, through her nutritionists activities came across the intestinal cleanse sometimes referred to as "The Lemonade Diet." At 6 foot 2 inches and approximately 190 pounds I appeared to be relatively fit for a 45-year-old guy. However, when I removed my shirt, what I saw in the mirror alarmingly began to resemble the profile of an expectant mother at about 4 months baked. Remember those painful and traumatic experiences I spoke of a minute ago? I suddenly found new motivation. You see I have a very petite, stunningly beautiful and amazingly youthful-looking wife and I'll be *damned* if anybody's ever gonna mistake me for her *father* or *older brother*. O Yeah, there was gonna be some changes Bro!

So I start this cleanse. Nothing but fresh squeezed lemon juice; pure maple syrup; cayenne pepper, and water mixed together. One 10-ounce glass, drank 6 or more times per day. That's it. Minimum recommendation of at least 10 days. I did fourteen. I started at 198lbs. I finished at 178lbs, and felt like I was about 25 years old. But this is the more exciting part. Every physical urge was quieted after about day 3. I gained total control for the first time ever, and had complete dominance over my body during that 14-day stretch. I prayed and exercised every morning and again each night before bed. The stomach dropped off and I had the beginning ripples of a "six-pack" when it was done.

All it takes is one significant victory to build your confidence and create enthusiasm for the fight against impure thoughts and other areas where you lack self-control or will power. This exercise became a new weapon for me. Whenever I begin to feel that my flesh is dictating too many of my actions such as over-eating, eating too much of the wrong food, or even yearning too much for sex with my spouse, I'll immediately go on a 2 or 3 day fast just to regain control. I also use this time to refocus and restore my spirit to a place of dominance within me.

I can tell when this happens because my thoughts and my mind will become refreshingly clear. I'm able to be at peace in my decision-making. I am much more sensitive and attuned to the needs of my wife and family. I even perform my job better at work and become more effective as a leader because I am not distracted mentally with thoughts of selfish fulfillment. I have more mental energy to devote toward prosperous endeavors and things that are beneficial and progressive in nature.

Sexual relations in a marriage is always a sensitive subject and can be very stressful from either side if communication is clouded and mutual expectations are not truthfully and lovingly expressed.

If a man has been engaging in pornography his sex drive has likely been over-stimulated. His idea of sexual activity has been heavily influenced by staged, edited and professionally acted scenes intentionally choreographed to achieve maximum erotic effects. Even though humans have the incredible ability to compartmentalize relationships, behaviors and emotions; there will be some things that attach themselves so deeply into your subconscious that they become your reality and your accepted norm. I know of men who request that their wives have sex wearing high heel shoes. Some others need to have their wives dress in provocative lingerie or other erotic costumes and perform strip-tease dances for them in order for the man to be "entertained" as a form of sexual foreplay. None of these things are sinful or bad behaviors. However, it is the *heart condition* which drives the need for such activity that must be examined.

I doubt that there are many "sexual education" booklets that depict the female wearing spiked heels and a "barely-there" nurse's outfit to demonstrate the act of lovemaking or sexual intercourse. Those images manifested in the man's mind from somewhere and my money is on some form of pornographic input.

My belief is that pornography falls into the same category of addiction as substance abuse like cocaine habits or alcoholism, because it acts as a source of mind control. After watching countless hours of sexually charged images your mind eventually begins to exist in an altered state. Just like with drunkenness or continual drug abuse, your judgment is impaired and the course of your life is being navigated without your total comprehension.

Until you clear your mind and body of the substance that is polluting it, you will never regain control of your destiny.

For many couples romantic or erotic role-playing can be an exciting departure from the mundane and when such things are done in mutual cooperation with an attitude of genuine desire to please one another, they can add spice and spontaneity to the relationship. The bible states that "The marriage is honorable in all and the bed undefiled: but whoremongers and adulterers God will judge." (Hebrews 13:4) I interpret this to mean that whatever a married man and woman mutually and willfully consent to, in regards to sex, is blessed under the marriage covenant, unless it is a practice that is clearly prohibited by God such as sodomy, incest or bestiality.

Whenever I find myself receiving almost unbearable impulses for sex in my marriage, I immediately assume or take the position that it is me who is out of control regardless to what my wife is or is not doing, or how long it has been since we were last intimate. I don't want my physical urges dictating anything that I do, whether it is eating, sexual activity or even too much sleeping. I try always to weigh the end result of the physical call, against the pressure of the call, to determine the true underlying motivation. For instance; if the end result of eating that piece of cake after a fairly large meal is going to result in my feeling sluggish, bloated and uncomfortable, then I am not going to accept it (no matter how persuasively it's offered to me.)

Here is another: If I know that sleeping past 10 o'clock usually causes me to wake up with a headache and feel regretful that a good portion of my day has gotten away, then I'm going to get up at 9 o'clock whether I have some place to go or not. In regard to sex, if I sense that my wife is fatigued, unable to focus or responding to me only due to "not-so-subtle" pressure from me to perform, then I am not going to force the issue because the end result is going to be an unfulfilling, one-sided, laborious event. I am not going to be fulfilled because my love for her necessitates that she be willingly and mutually engaged in the process. Complete pleasure for me is in pleasing her and I in turn receive attention and passion from her that expresses the same desire towards me.

Please understand that this was not the case for the larger portion of our years together. This only started to come about as I began to apply a second strategy of squelching my roving eye for pornographic input.

Singleness of focus

God's word states that […if the eye be single, the body will be full of light.] (Matthew

6:22 Para.) Spiritually this refers to God and His Word being the object of your focused eye and the light being revelatory knowledge and understanding. For the non-believer we can find common ground if you can get with the notion that God's word translates into universal principles, which you adopt and operate within on a daily basis. Principles as obvious as gravity or as complex and multi-dimensional as sowing and reaping.

I chose as a strategy to make my wife the object of my single focus and the light of revelation would begin to reveal to me her true value and the significance of her presence in my life. I found perfect parallels between God's scriptures and true-to-life tangible manifestations in my marriage. When I place my focus on God and His Word, my attention to other problems and worrisome situations are for that period of time made less significant and they're less able to occupy my mind's energy.

When I began to place my focus on pleasing my wife before and above myself and being more mindful of issues concerning her life, my own personal needs began to consume less of my mental energy. This accordingly began to reduce the power of the call of my flesh to command my attention. The power of the flesh is maximized when your mind is idle and devoid of a purpose or a goal that draws from within you and requires the full participation of your mental capacity and emotional drive. The need to view pornographic material became less and less significant because the object of my focus was placed more appropriately on my spouse until finally pornography felt more like a distant memory.

I would literally place pictures of my wife in every area that I could. If I had to have any image in my mind other than a goal, a project or a purpose, I wanted it to be her and her alone. This not only is my most effective tool against porn or any other lustful thoughts, but it had the added benefit of increasing my passion and appreciation for my wife in ways I never imagined.

By the end of the day I can hardly wait to see her because I've been gazing at her all day, at my desk, on the sun-visor of my car, in my day planner, etc., etc. (It doesn't hurt that she's a real *looker* too.)

The power of fear

The power of fear is a third tactic when used as a motivator. Fear can work for or against you. It works against you if it has you trapped in secrecy. You fear exposure, embarrassment, humiliation, loss of relationships or positions of power, or loss of status. However if you've chosen to strip the power of the enemy to paralyze you with fear by going on the attack and confessing your problem, you now have something new to fear which should be viewed positively. That is the fear of disappointment; disappointment in yourself. You may also fear disappointing those who have supported and forgiven you. Much like a substance abuser who has tried to quit and then fallen "off the wagon" again and again, people will soon tire of being lied to and any attempts of yours to regain trust will be futile. Unlike drug addiction though, I believe pornography is viewed with much less sympathy and tolerance. It is greeted with more disgust because it is not a physical dependency but a moral weakness and a sleazy habit.

It carries an aura of nastiness and perversity that many women find hard to accept as something that a man is not capable of controlling. This I totally understand because as earlier stated they are not moved by the same physical stimulus as men.

To a woman this activity screams of weakness and whether spoken or unspoken; no woman wants to be lead by, or can truly respect a weak man. It goes against her inherent instincts to seek security and protection for herself and her children. How can she feel secure if you're a weakling in character and sound judgment? How can she trust her future to your hands if you're not even capable of keeping your hands off of yourself? These words are not meant to injure or insult you my brothers but to quicken you to the harsh realities of this game of secrecy. In this sport the ladies hate "the game" and "the Playa."

In my life there are many people who are now becoming aware and more who have yet to find out of this secret life I've lived. Most will probably be understanding, you know, "let him who is without sin cast the first stone" and so forth. Some may not understand and privately or publicly despise me as a fraud or just another religious perpetrator who deserves no leniency. I'll take whatever comes. What I cannot take is the look of shame and disappointment on the faces of those who love and have forgiven me if I should fall again and return to this shameful habit. So I use the fear of seeing those faces as a tool or a weapon against any darts of temptation that the enemy might throw my way.

If there is no one in your life whom if disappointed, would evoke such a response from you, then this concept would obviously be ineffective for you. That possibility is more likely to exist in the life of a single man.

However, *"The fear of the Lord is the beginning of wisdom."* (Psalms 111:10) If you are a believer there should be nothing and no one you have greater fear and reverence for than God. To add further emphasis; *"The fear of the Lord prolongs days, but the years of the wicked will be shortened."* (Proverbs 10:27) also; *"The fear of the Lord leads to life, and he who has it will abide in satisfaction."* (Proverbs 19:23). The Lord, through access to His infinite devices, has the ability to satisfy you spiritually, emotionally and physically if you will submit your will to worship, honor and adhere to His ways.

This fear of which I speak is not that of dread or of punishment for wicked behavior, but it is something born out of the deepest love, respect and worshipful acknowledgement for the Lord of all creation, whose thoughts and desires towards us are of goodness beyond what we can even conceive.

Our reverence for God should be such that it upholds our integrity as individuals even when there is no other human being in our lives to whom we owe such honor and respect as to fear their disappointment.

Get a life

This fourth strategy deals directly with the destructive impact of porn addiction on your life. To quote a phrase "the idle mind is a playground for the devil." No truer words were ever spoken. If I could lump together every minute I've ever spent occupying my mind with pornography and sum it up with one title it would be "Life Lost." As my Pastor once stated, life is too short to devote any of my time to anything that is going to be unfruitful. How much further in life could I have potentially been if I had used those minutes, hours and days applying my mind towards something that might've benefited my family, myself or mankind in a meaningful way? A sense of purpose is one of the most powerful forces that a human being can possess.

This is another reason why we must gain a basic understanding of how we as humans are made to function. If you're struggling to whip pornography and have been for a long time, stop and examine your overall mental focus. What are you committed to accomplishing that is larger than your own ability to achieve? What mark do you desire to leave on this world? How many lives are being affected for the better because of you or because of your ideas, creations, inventions or your personal involvement?

I guarantee that if you'll begin to ask yourself these types of questions and diligently seek a cause or a personal dream to pursue, you'll see the physical call of pornography begin to weaken and start to lose it's stronghold over your mind. When you willingly sacrifice your time and energy to add value to the lives of others, just the fulfillment of giving and being a blessing carries its own reward.

This is the driving force behind this book. I am grieved by the loss of life I've foolishly inflicted on myself and I felt compelled to do what I could to help others work through this problem. I am now getting an understanding of the incredible scope of this hideous mind infection on the men of this world society.

I cannot possibly close out this chapter without including a fifth and most critical tool that is indispensable in battling this weakness of moral character; the **_Connection with God_** whom I consider to be the origin of the ultimate standard of moral values. I humbly appeal to those readers who may not confess a belief in Christ to consider that there are an infinite number of things or realities that cannot be explained by man or reasoned away with logic. There are a lifetime of writings and other paraphernalia designed to evangelize and expose the loving kindness of our Lord to you. While I proudly proclaim my faith in the God of the Bible and belief in His Son Jesus Christ as my savior, I choose not to make that the focus of my interaction with you through these pages. I will simply try to convey this concept in plain and simple non-religious terminology because my mission is to benefit anyone from any walk of life by sharing my experiences and my testimony. However, I do recognize that a non-believer will find it more difficult to give credence to the power available from some unseen, intangible source.

If anyone has tried to overcome some form of pornography using just will-power or the power of their own internal voice to control their thoughts and thereby their actions, you will have discovered by now that it is going to take something stronger than you. If you're honest with yourself, you'll also have to admit that there is something very significant missing in your life. That "something" may go by a variety of names; happiness, peace, contentment, serenity or fulfillment to name just a few. Another term I like to use is called "grace." One biblical definition of grace is "God's unmerited favor." I like to think of grace as an external power source that I can draw from which also acts as a covering. Because I see God as my Creator and my Father, I trust that I can look to Him for assistance when I'm unable to support myself.

When I was a child, I often found ways to get myself into situations that I did not know how to get out of. I would invariably wind up going to dad to fix it or for back up. Even though it was my screw-up, because He loved me His compassion would arise and His mercy would be granted toward me. He would come to my aid because of His loving desire not to see me struggle or be burdened with more than I could bear.

On the flipside of that, if I refused my Father's help He would be powerless to assist me no matter how much He wanted to, or how much it pained Him to see me going through the fire. His love and all the power of His resources would not cease to exist, but because I refused to acknowledge them, they would not be available to me. If there is total darkness in my house, though I might be surrounded by lamps with perfectly working bulbs, if I never plug them into an electrical socket their light is not available for me. This is exactly the case concerning God's power and grace, and the non-believer. How can you possibly benefit from His resources if you consciously refuse His assistance by denying that He even exists?

I pray that as you continue to read these pages, the spirit of God will connect with your spirit and inspire you to willfully and joyfully acknowledge His existence and to accept His Son as your personal Lord and Savior.

CHAPTER 6 – **PORNOGRAPHY AND THE SINGLE GUY**

Now in the case of you single fellas, you'll probably need to begin with tool #5 and work backwards because you'll likely be needing some serious supernatural assistance.

If you're single and living alone, you lack the advantages of many of the built-in blockers to pornography that we married guys have. There is no spouse or significant other living with you that you have to hide your porn stash from. If you have Internet access, you've got a 24 hour a day window into the limitless world of filth. You've got a plethora of cable channels showing adult films at your request. You most likely don't deal with the fear of any children accidentally stumbling across your stash or into some XXX-Rated website that you left open on your computer. You don't have to account to anyone for your whereabouts or for your spending habits.

So in reality you must establish for yourself your own extremely high standard of moral integrity because there is no real threat to your privacy being breached and in the secure realm of that privacy, there is nothing preventing you from indulging as much as you'd like accept your own integrity and self-discipline. The fortification of your mind and your conscious will is extremely vital. Many of the emotional factors which come into play within the dynamics of marital relations, are not present for the single person. There is no one else's life that will be directly affected by your illicit practices.

I know of a guy who operates a business out of his home, a recording studio to be exact. This fella is married and has two small children. When working at his studio, one time I went to use his washroom, which was in his basement as was the studio. To my astonishment, when I entered the bathroom, I immediately noticed that he had a rack of pornographic magazines sitting right next to the toilet. I had never before seen a situation like this where a wife with two children freely roaming their small house would stand for that or accept it without a major fight. My mind couldn't even conceive of such a thing.

I had never been so uncomfortable and conflicted, being faced with the flagrant display of my secret vice. Instead of getting a thrill at an opportunity to peruse a little porn openly, I was more embarrassed and a bit disgusted by it. I might have been a secret porno-dipping sinner, but I could never have disrespected my wife or exposed my children to my wretched habit in that way. Here was a case of a married man treating his home as if he were single under the pretense I'd imagine of catering to his "rocker" clientele. I don't believe that there is any way a man who is not indulging in pornography would allow for something like that, especially not in his own home. In hindsight, I think that this should have served more for me as a sad example of the degree to which pornography had become acceptable in our society, rather than an indictment of one man and the depth of his sin verses my own.

I must admit that I have great sympathy for the single male and I'm instinctually less judgmental in regard to their falling prey to pornography.

Yes, the male sex drive is a force to be reckoned with and it's probably about a thousand times more intense for the man who is not even romantically involved and has few or no prospects on the horizon. I know that the religious and biblically correct thing for me to say right about now would be for you guys to just seek God through His Word and set your heart upon serving and pleasing Him. After all when we confess Christ as Lord, we symbolically and spiritually sacrifice our will for His will and vow to live for Him and He will abide in us. He thereby empowers us with His strength, His righteousness and His grace that is sufficient to keep us chaste and having the capacity to practice self-restraint and live holy according to His commandments.

But again, for the non-believer this is simply not enough in the face of the sensual onslaught of erotic imagery coming against his senses each and every day. He's left having to do something to relieve that sexual tension that has no human counterpart towards whom it can be focused. Trying to deny that it exists will only lead to frustration and inner turmoil.

To prove that society recognizes this reality we have even created electronic and manual devices or "toys" for women that are designed to relieve their sexual urges or to provide a form of self-stimulation and relaxation. For women we politely snicker and look past it as sort of an unspoken, non-issue. But for the male we give it the unseemly title of "masturbation" and prohibit it with the threat of blindness or eternal damnation if you participate in it. How unfair is that?

No my single friends, I cannot find it within me to judge you too harshly knowing for myself the mind-warping power of this physical pull on the flesh. The Bible states that it is better to marry than to burn with lust. (I Corinthians 7:9 Para.) I find it significant that the bible uses the descriptive term 'burn' in characterizing this physical phenomenon.

I can recall when I first heard the phrase "in heat." It was used in reference to an animal such as a dog or cat that had reached a period or a season in its life where it was physically driven to mate with the opposite sex of its species, or it caused extreme pain and discomfort. These animals were sometimes driven to violence or uncharacteristically erratic behavior that could appear as much mental as physical during these periods. I believe this almost perfectly describes the impulses that can afflict humans as well. The critical difference being, we are a higher level of creation than animals. Animals, whether in the wild or domesticated are not self-aware or capable of insightful thinking. Their actions where sex is concerned are completely driven by pre-programmed instincts. They do not possess the ability to completely reverse or change the course of their lives or who they are by simply deciding to do so. We humans can make the decision to change and then to re-structure our total environment in order to bring the desired change to pass.

This is why I must insist to my single brothers that yes, even you are capable of abstaining from self-stimulation and the habit of pornography if you're willing to tap into the spiritual power within you. I did not say nor would I ever imply that I thought it would be easy to overcome but I know and have proven for myself that the flesh can be subdued and made to conform to the guidelines and standards that you have consciously set, sub-consciously programmed and physically disciplined yourself to carry out.

I have read where one well known pastor had stated that he would not even ride alone in an elevator with a woman other than his wife. I also know of other ministers and pastors that will not meet or do one-on-one counseling alone with a woman in their offices, with the door closed, or without a secretary nearby. They've adopted these radical practices, not only to avoid the appearance of any impropriety, but also to prohibit the opportunity for their flesh to be tempted to sin out of lust. Many morally conscientious doctors will not examine a female patient alone in an examining room without a female nurse present.

Measures such as these may seem extreme but they are crucial and must be imposed if you ever hope to succeed in the daily battle against lustful thoughts that feed inappropriate sexual urges.

For men who travel often, when staying alone in hotel rooms, it is possible to phone ahead or specify when making reservations that you are requesting there be no adult movie programming accessible to your room under any circumstances. The same applies to in-home cable services. Get blockers or filters on your Internet service that will deny access to websites that offer x-rated or adult content.

If you regularly pass by a magazine stand or an adult video and bookstore that you used to frequent you may need to change your travel routes in order to avoid arousing old impulses triggered by familiar environments. Be extremely mindful of your conscious thoughts and in what directions your thoughts tend to be pulled by certain situations that you observe.

Another very important variable is your speech. Be conscious of what you say and of what you allow yourself to listen to and absorb. Throughout my life, I've had several friends and acquaintances that seemed to have very different values and standards than those I had. There is a passage of scripture that speaks of how [...evil communications corrupt good manners]. (I Corinthians 15:33) Or simply put, if you customarily surround yourself with people who speak negatively and habitually use profane language, odds are you will eventually begin to speak and think the same way. It almost never happens the other way around. Certain types of unfiltered, mindless speech can over time begin to erode your standard of what level of conversation is appropriate and acceptable. If the dialogue is constantly laced with profanity, lewd sexual references or content that is useless, unimportant or devoid of substance overall, it's probably wise to steer clear of it.

You must be of the mind to do whatever is necessary to control your environment and to heavily scrutinize what kind of input is received into your eyes and ears. It is up to you to defend these access points with every method of defense that can be employed.

Another consideration that needs to be examined is the value level at which you place the female gender. Is a woman simply an object to be used as stimulus for you or is she something to be cherished and appreciated.

My pastor has often stated that the best time to look for or to entertain the notion of a companion is when you really don't need one. When you're content, well-balanced and whole as an individual, you are less likely to act out of desperation or weakness when making the selection of whom to be with. However, is it better to marry than to burn with lust? Yes it is. Is there any circumstance under which self-stimulation is acceptable? In my humble opinion the answer is also, yes. If the yearning for sexual activity has overwhelmed your consciousness to the degree that your main motivation for connecting with someone is to fill the void for sexual fulfillment or physical intimacy, I say self-stimulation is an appropriate option. This may appear to conflict with my earlier statements but hear me out. I believe that the reason a device or a "toy" can be created for a woman's self-stimulation, and it not become a cultural obsession, is because a woman is (in general) better able to distinguish and to separate the physical need for it, from the deeper sub-conscious and emotional need for it. I believe that they are able to disconnect from the erotic aspect which is an essential component for the man.

    I believe that women can focus in on the physical benefits of sexual release that could tend to build up and manifest as stress from prolonged periods of inactivity, without becoming a slave to it or requiring pornographic images to facilitate it. It's like the famed "Calgon bath" that temporarily "takes them away" to a place of relaxation and stress relief. However, when it's over, it's over and it's back to the real world and the handling of real world issues.

I think men are vastly different. We are much more visual creatures and we can be driven by the passions that are evoked by those images. Since women are primarily the focus of those images (at least they should be), your comfort level with how they are portrayed, will be established in correlation with the value you place on them. Let me pose it this way; if every porno flick or website you viewed showed only women that resembled your mom, your sister, your daughter or some other woman that was very dear to you, how aroused could you get? Then let's suppose she was being forcefully dominated by several men at once. Could you in any way be turned on by that, or would you be horrified by it? My guess would be the latter. It would likely be due to the emotional attachment and the value you have for those particular women. Did it occur to you that every woman is a sister, a daughter or a mother to someone?

I found that this concept was made even more meaningful and given more weight when the idea of a holy and loving God was added to the equation, and I was given access to His value system through my willful acceptance of Him. Through the study of His Word and learning of His ways I was able to look at the female gender through His (their Creator's) eyes and to learn to appreciate and esteem them in the image as originally intended by Him. The beauty of their creation and the immeasurable depth of their purpose was brought to light within me. Once I began to meditate on the notion of a woman as God sees her and I gave His will preeminence above my own will, I found that I was also more empowered to dominate my thought life. It is much more difficult to lower my thoughts into lusting after a woman if I view her with the same value as the women I most highly esteem and treasure in my own life.

For the single man, the development of a grand respect and admiration for women as the precious treasure that they are, will greatly assist you in your mental battle against pornography. As an added benefit it will also make you a better lover when you do marry. Even during the courtship phase you'll be more attractive to your mate because she'll detect your sincere appreciation for her as a woman and not get the feeling of being just a sex object to you.

Begin to envision your life a year or two from now. How do you desire to look in the eyes of the woman you hope to marry? Are you in the best possible position that you could be to accommodate and support her life? Could your finances stand any improvement? Are you emotionally stable and settled in your lifestyle or do you still like the variety and freedom of a carefree life, without having to consider the opinions or feelings of a spouse? Is a spiritual life important to you and how well rooted are you in your faith? Do you have a solid plan and vision for your future that you are in the process of carrying out and do you believe that this vision is inspiring and attractive enough to appeal to the kind of woman that you desire?

If you get to work building sound answers to questions like these, you'll find that there is plenty with which to occupy your mind and your time instead of lusting after shapely bodies and stimulating yourself blind with pornography.

It's quite interesting to think of how much truth is in that bit of humor about the fear of "going blind" from masturbation. There is much deeper revelation to be uncovered there. Habitual indulgence in porn or an unbridled obsession or lust for any form of sexual activity, can have the effect of clouding your mind. You begin to find that everything you see and hear takes the form of a sexual connotation. You're constantly thinking of possible opportunities for an encounter with someone you find attractive or whom you think may be willing or available. Every shapely figure or flash of exposed skin catches your eye to the point of distraction. Your attention span gets shorter, because your concentration is interrupted constantly by little subliminal news bulletins reminding you of your craving. Not for food like normal over-weight, beef inhaling, diet coke drinking, pie-hole stuffing, red-blooded Americans. No, you want something that absolutely makes no rational sense; to spend life's precious ever-decreasing moments, stroking away the hours in some fictitious mental fantasy-land, where beautiful people allow you to pull-up a chair and just gaze at them in every manner of sexual perversity.

While you're locked away indulging your particular vice, imagine that your next-door neighbor is into child pornography and at the same time, the guy across the street is into watching young boys being sodomized or women being tortured while raped. Is there much difference between them and you? Well of course there is; you only watch consenting adults, right? Well how about consenting bi-sexual adults or transvestite sex?

Once you've opened yourself up to pornography you start to develop an increasing appetite very rapidly. Just like a drug addict you will build up a tolerance level for pornographic images and they will have to grow more and more vivid and usually more wicked and depraved in order to bring you to a heightened state of arousal. I would imagine that most men who practice in the aforementioned vices did not start out at that depth of depravity. They likely evolved to that point through years of indulgence to the sin. It's all an abomination to God at most and a gross violation of our own human dignity at the least. It really doesn't matter which perverted preference you choose.

The poor misguided or victimized soul being directed on the screen is not the real issue. The issue is, what has happened to your moral standard? At what point did images such as these not only cease to disturb you, but become a source of erotic stimulation for you? If you're even able to trace back to that point in time, you'll start to see just how much of your life has been wasted and how blinded you've been to the fact that it was slipping away from you, or better stated, being stolen from you.

If you, yes *You* single guy, ever hope to someday marry, and ask a wonderful woman to walk out life's journey according to your dreams, you have an obligation to stay clean. You'll do wise to walk in righteousness and live with moral integrity, preparing yourself to be worthy of the awesome gift of her love and devotion to you. You <u>CAN</u> Do It! (You single stud you.)

CHAPTER 7 – **SHE LOVES ME....SHE LOVES ME NOT**

To the wife of the porn addicted man, I must first assure you that it is <u>not your fault</u>. You can stuff your dressers and chests with the equivalent of an entire Victoria's Secret Spring & Summer edition and it would not be an answer to his problem. I don't know whether you'd find it painful or more of a relief but understand that it really has little to do with you. Oh, to be sure, if you're having marital problems, money problems, children problems or just a lot of stress in the home, it makes it that much easier for him to mentally escape into his world of erotica. However, the root causes are to be found deeper within his mind and it was probably implanted much earlier in his life by some person, some image or some event that had a profound impact on his sub-conscious mind. For me it was the discovery of that porn magazine when my immature little mind was ill-equipped to handle such stimulating data.

Mothers don't be deceived. There is a reason why the promoters of homosexual rights and "alternative lifestyles" are bucking to get into the schools with their educational agenda at as early an age as possible. There are reasons why some clothing companies have been known to target their ads to young audiences using youthful looking models in various degrees of undress and posed in very sexually suggestive, gender neutral types of scenes. There are reasons why the film, television and music industries have grown much more bold and deliberate with their sexually provocative movies and "R-rated" dialogue, to the point where no TV program is safe for young, easily influenced eyes and ears. Even if the program is reasonably tame, you still cannot relax, because practically every other commercial has some scantily clad *Barbie doll* as the focus of the ad. The magicians of subliminal seduction within the media, the educational system and the TV/Film industries fully understand the power of a brief but emotionally stimulating message on the subconscious mind, especially an immature or uninformed and unsuspecting mind. The impressions made in a moment can establish a paradigm that will guide him unawares, for the rest of his life.

So yes indeed mom, guard your sons and daughter's hearts and minds with all diligence because what is deposited in them while young will mold their lives and if corrupt will set them on a path of destruction that may take years to reverse.

If your man is like most dealing with this infection, the odds are very great that he can recall a pivotal moment in his formative years that awakened a hornet's nest of emotions he was not equipped to process appropriately.

It is understandable that you will probably experience a range of emotions from anger to hurt to disbelief. You are absolutely entitled to those feelings. But if you love him and have decided to support him through the process of overcoming this issue, then your response to him after the exposing of his habit will immeasurably effect whether he starts toward the road to deliverance or becomes even more indifferent because of a punishing sense of loss, rejection and failure.

No, you cannot be expected to be his cure or his savior but if he truly loves you and is determined not to lose you, your forgiveness and willingness to ride out the storm, believing that he is capable of victory, will be absolutely critical toward his success.

No one knows with absolute certainty what to expect as you enter into marriage. I truly believe that no one is "set-up" for a disastrous relationship as some sort of punishment by God. He gave us the power of choice and you chose to be with the partner you have. Now you must believe that He has equipped you with His Grace and that it is sufficient to enable you to see beyond your husband's weaknesses, to the man of honor and integrity that God created him to be. Show him that you believe that he is "that" man. Express to him how deeply he has hurt you, but that in spite of his actions, you will allow him the opportunity to redeem himself and to regain your trust. Be sure, however, to make clear your expectations and feel free to let him know that you will not be mocked or made a fool of repeatedly. If he is not willing to change or to acknowledge his problem he must understand that there will be consequences.

Man is capable of reaching such depths of sin and depravity that even God can be forced to give him over to his own lusts and willful disobedience, which will lead to self-destruction. Your spouse must be made to recognize what he stands to lose if he does not actively seek assistance or personally takes whatever steps necessary to overcome his addiction.

CHAPTER 8 – **THE SINS OF THE FATHER**

When the president of the United States was discovered to have had oral sex in the oval office of the Whitehouse with a young female intern the entire nation was rocked by scandal. Our country was made a laughing stock to the other nations of the world and the highest office in the land was sullied in a manner that cut to the heart of many patriotic Americans, who hold a belief that the occupant of that office must adhere to a higher standard of moral integrity than that of average citizens.

When professional athletes, actors, government officials and especially religious leaders of the day are found to be morally deficient and severely lacking in ethical character, does anyone take measure of the impact on our younger citizens and the subsequent decline of morals and standards in generations that follow? I'm certain that some have and that there is an abundance of statistical data to that effect clogging up someone's computer hard drive somewhere. However, how do you calculate the impact on the sons and daughters of those caught in the act and exposed to the blaring light of public scrutiny?

How does the President sit down as a father and explain to his daughter how he was compelled to engage in a sex act with a woman not many years older than her? How does he maintain any dignity and self-respect in her eyes? How does he explain his rationale for humiliating her mother this way and bringing shame and ridicule on the family? How does the star athlete caught in adultery or fathering other children out-of-wedlock explain to his young son that he shouldn't mistreat his mother without feeling like a complete hypocrite? Unfortunately, the fear of being confronted with these and many other such heart-wrenching questions is not reserved for only Presidents, star athletes or high-profile people.

As I write this book my children are entering adulthood and are old enough to comprehend the subject matter in discussion. I dealt with the topic of pornography with my son some time ago and informed him of my experience with it as a fatherly warning of what to stay away from with all diligence.

With my daughter, who is the older of the two, I touched on the subject briefly when she inquired as to the topic of my book. Fortunately, I believe we have established a relationship that is capable of withstanding such a revelation. Also fortunate is that my children have lived through the reparation stages of our marriage and though they've witnessed the occasional heated argument, all they know for certain is that their Dad loves their Mom more than life itself and that they're not breakin' up for nothin'!

Nevertheless, those same concerns haunted me for years and added to the power of the stronghold of secrecy that I was under. Every father wants to have the respect and admiration of his children. I have the utmost respect for my Dad. As a child and a young man, I always knew that I could count on him for support and consistency. I've watched how he's loved and cared for my mother and now in his golden years my hope is that I will be a support for them in whatever capacity they need. My Dad has always been a man of integrity and he remains highly respected by his peers and associates.

This also serves to prove to me that pornography addiction is not necessarily a result of your up-bringing or environment. The seed of perversion may be planted in childhood at some point, but it is much more of a 'personal choice' addiction. Over-stimulation through visual erotica is not some new epidemic. It has always been and will always be around us. Opportunities to be exposed to it may be more abundant through more options of media today, but we as individuals still have the ultimate responsibility to police what we allow into our consciousness.

That's why it is so very important that we as parents monitor what kinds of input our children are being exposed to. My parents did an admirable job of keeping risqué magazines out of the house and adult movie channels off of the cable TV package. How could they know that my mind had been so corrupted as to compel me to "make the decision" to view pornographic material? My own lusts drove me to manipulate the cable signal to pick up adult movie programming. Those were my choices. What is extremely tormenting to the porn addict is to be fully aware of the threat and haunted with the fear of being exposed and subjected to horrifying humiliation; and yet to still feel powerless to defy the temptation of sexual lust. I have known this torment.

I imagine that little else could devastate me more than to lose the respect and admiration of my children in a manner that could forever cripple my ability to be a positive influence in their lives.

If they no longer regard me as honorable or to be held in high esteem, what value would my words possibly hold for them? If your children don't see their connection with you as a source of pride, they will shrink from association with you and you will become ineffective as a father figure. A young person's self-esteem and confidence are constantly under attack via pressure from peers and societal fads, to conform to their dictates of what is acceptable, desirable or "in" at the time. They need stability and self-assurance which they should be able to draw from you as their father and their source of security. If your stature crumbles into ashes before their eyes and in a way that opens them up to ridicule and scorn, you will be seen as responsible for the collapse of their life's foundational structure. That could take a lifetime to recover from. No child deserves such a burden. No family deserves to be so callously and wastefully torn apart and brought to shame.

I desperately admonish any father reading these pages that values his children and his family, to adopt the techniques mentioned in this book or any other methods that will empower you to rid yourself of this mental and spiritual virus. Some form of psychiatric or spiritual counseling may be necessary if you feel that you are beyond the levels of addiction described in this book.

If you don't feel lead to do it for yourself, do it to benefit the ones you love.

CHAPTER 9 – **TAKE THE RISK**

If the thought of losing the life you have evokes you to fear, it must be worth taking a risk to hold on to.

There are two things of which I am certain regarding the addiction to pornography; as long as it is kept in secrecy, you will never defeat it; and until you take the risk of revealing it, you will never know how much time you've lost needlessly living in fear and torment, because you never trusted the ones you love to love you enough to forgive you. My marriage today is so amazingly fulfilling because I now know the depths of my wife's love for me. Not that I had any reason to question it before, but the bondage of fear and shame is so powerful that it has the effect of paranoia and through self-condemnation, can make you feel pitiful and unworthy of love or forgiveness. She only confirmed her love by sticking with me through the lowest points in my life, and by faith, believing that the man she expected to spend the rest of her life with, was still in here somewhere and that he would eventually re-surface and become all that she believed he would.

By not being exposed I lived with the risk of never being free of guilt and fear; the risk of living a miserable, tortured existence as an empty and dysfunctional human being. Yes, you can potentially stand to lose everything by confessing your problem. Depending on your status level or position in life, a "stepping down" may be temporarily required; however, this can be handled discretely and privately if you are in control of the degree and scope of the exposure. If it is uncovered in a public way, you lose all power of control and the ensuing scandal may cause greater pain to your spouse and family than if you had been honest and confessed to her. Ultimately, you must weigh the cost and calculate the risk.

I believe that a humble and contrite spirit invokes the grace of God and that you will find an unexpected receptiveness and forgiveness for your vices. If you are truly repentant and your loved ones can perceive that you are, they will most likely have some empathy for you and not wish to heap further condemnation upon you. You must also exercise a measure of faith and know that in the end, the truth being brought to light is always preferable to living a lie and attempting to lead a double life. The power of truth, goodness and integrity will provoke the gift of mercy to be directed toward you.

This sentiment can be thought of as the main theme of this book if there is to be one. I strongly believe that the fear of disclosure is the ultimate grip that binds and enslaves you to this life of secrecy. The pressure of the self-condemnation and sense of failure can be so powerful as to evoke thoughts of suicide or to bring the onset of severe depression.

By refusing to take the risk, you choose to continue in a life of lies, deceit, sinfulness, unfaithfulness and weakness that doesn't pan out to be much of a life at all. When I weigh what I've "given up" so to speak, against the peace, self-esteem, sense of empowerment and restored righteousness that I now have, there is really no question that it was well worth the risk to come clean. Many who are reading this book who have known me for years, are learning of this other, darker side to my past. Some of you may feel a sense of disappointment, disillusionment, shock or maybe nothing at all because you think everybody's doing it anyway. I can only tell you that it was worth the exposure to now qualify to hold whatever level of respect or admiration that you held for me. I find that the more open and honest I am about the secret past I've lived, the more victorious I feel over this mental dysfunction called pornography and the more empowered I feel to hopefully assist others in rising out of this dark life.

In the end, only you can determine whether it's worth the risk to expose your vice and lay yourself open for the world to judge. If it helps at all, just know that you're never alone whichever side of the decision you're on. You'll have plenty of company amongst those who choose to maintain their secrecy, perhaps waiting for the ever elusive "right moment" before taking that leap of faith. I for one will be cheering you on in the hope that you'll decide to be free of the bondage you've endured for too long.

I believe you'll find that life is much sweeter on the other side of darkness.

CHAPTER 10 — **YOU DESERVE THE BEST**

You were created for a purpose. When the purpose of a thing is not known, abuse of that thing is inevitable. Pornography and other forms of sexual lasciviousness are hideous distortions of the physical aspects of human intercourse, which were originally designed to express our love in the most intimate manner and also to procreate the species. Fallen man has glorified the act of sex and all but stripped it of anything resembling the essence of the love of God.

The truest and most complete expression of Love is when it is reciprocal. Love is best and most gratifying when it is given away. It needs an object or an individual to be focused upon and released. God said after man's creation that it is not good that he should be alone. God in His perfect wisdom knew that just as He desired a *being* toward which to express His love, man, who is made in His likeness and possessing His nature, would also need such a *being*. In order to be most fulfilling and meaningful, the "Love target" must be equally capable of giving and receiving the same depth of love. A human can love a pet dog or cat but their pet cannot reciprocate that love in a way that is equal to the human. This is why God had to make Adam a companion that was suitable in every way for him to express his love toward, who could in return show him an equal degree of love. One who could match him in their capacity and capability to express the nature of his love physically, emotionally, intellectually and spiritually.

Just as it would be a gross distortion for a human being to attempt intimate sexual relations with an animal, it is no less a distortion for a man to engage in intimate sexual relations with himself. "It is not good for man to be alone." My assumption is that this means in a physical sexual manner also. If you are honest with yourself and truthfully examine your lifestyle of pornography indulgence, you'll begin to see that many other areas of your life have subtly become dysfunctional or distorted in some way.

You are living your life at an extremely low level and you're becoming oblivious to the reality of your low-life existence. You deserve better; but only if _you_ believe you do. I've heard it said that the average person typically functions at less than 10% of their mental capacity and overall level of potential. Well if that's the case for the average person, who's not suffering under some sort of addiction, just imagine how little you're operating on if a significant amount of your time and mental energy is being wasted on this meaningless, depressing and hedonistic sexual fantasy world you've been consumed by. Again I say; *You deserve better*, but only if _you_ believe you do.

I now know that it's a slap-in-the-face and a shameful insult to my Creator to abuse the gift of my life in such a disgraceful manner as this.

To paraphrase one of my Pastor's recent statements: "There is enough power in the Word of God to deliver you from any earthly circumstance." I would add, that you must first have *faith* in His Word in order to receive deliverance from Him. The key to the establishment of such faith is your sense of righteousness or right standing with Him. If you focus on your actions or sinful thoughts and behavior you will feel hopelessly condemned and ashamed before God. Trust His Word when it says, "If we confess our sin, He is faithful and just to forgive us our sins, and to cleanse us from all unrighteousness." (I John 1:9)

Don't even consider yourself as being able to earn God's acceptance or forgiveness based on how good you act, or how cleanly you try to live. He says that all our "self-righteousness is like filthy rags" to Him. (Isaiah 64:6) You simply have to know and trust that if you are in covenant with Him and accept His Son (Jesus) as your Lord and Savior, from then on, He sees you as righteous because of the sacrifice of Jesus and positioned in "right-standing" due to your brotherly association with Him. [...we are joint-heirs with Christ] (Romans 8:17)

God calls us to [awake to righteousness and sin not....] (I Corinthians 15:34) I interpret this to mean that when you regard yourself as having the stature befitting a son of royalty; along with that comes a level of dignity and self-worth that will prohibit you from engaging in any behavior or activity that typifies low morals or low-life standards.

Pornography addiction or any other type of addiction reduces you to low-life status because it strips you of all dignity and self-esteem.

You must begin to rebuild your image of who you are. If your childhood or past experiences have robbed you of a sense of identity, then you have the opportunity now to erase that old life and start anew. God's Word says that "Any man who is in Christ is a new creature; old things are passed away; behold, all things are become new." (II Corinthians 5:17) In order to break free of old habits, thoughts or paradigms, you may have to make a radical departure from your normal patterns of life. If you have never espoused any particular faith, I cannot think of anything more radical than to accept Christ as Lord of your life and to use His foundational teachings and principles as a launch pad for a new declaration of who you are, and the new path you intend to walk.

In order to sustain the progress that you'll begin to make, you'll have to continually work on your self-image and be in a constant mode of increasing and reaffirming your self-worth. The power you'll derive from the word of God, by faith, will build you up on the inside first and then strength of character will manifest on the outside. Don't expect to "feel" any different right away. Take it one day and one moment or one thought at a time. The next and last chapter will deal with the practical day-to-day techniques to use in reconditioning your mind and identifying the traps and triggers that lead you into lustful thoughts.

"Reverent and worshipful fear of the Lord is a fountain of life, that one may avoid the snare of death." (Proverbs 14:27- amp.)

CHAPTER 11 — **YOUR MIND: THE BATTLEFIELD**

"To the pure (in heart and conscience) all things are pure, but to the defiled and corrupt and unbelieving nothing is pure; their very minds and consciences are defiled and polluted." (Titus 1:15 amp.)

All actions begin as a single thought. There are some physical reactions that may occur as an impulse such as blinking or flinching when an object approaches your eyes unexpectedly. However, our conscious decisions to act do not fall into that category. The Bible says that if a married man looks (meditates continuously) upon a woman in lust you have already committed adultery in your heart. (Matthew 5:28) This points out how dangerous it is to allow even the thought of wickedness to linger in your mind.

Until you are able to reign-in the thoughts that infiltrate your mind you will never have any sustainable success in the battle to overcome porn addiction.

You can begin by becoming acutely conscious of the moments that you're first stimulated or the impulse to view pornography is triggered. What were you looking at or listening to? Who were you talking to and what was the topic of conversation? Be as painstakingly precise and honest as possible in tracing the original thought. Mentally step outside yourself and think like a detective, as if your life depended on it. Once you identify the source of the thought or the trigger, now you can determine which techniques to employ to nullify those thoughts. Each time you perform this exercise you'll grow in resistance and there will be fewer and fewer traps that can affect you as you begin to catalog them and build-up your defenses against them.

If you notice that you're listening to a particular radio show as you drive each day that tends to veer into somewhat racy subject matter, then you may need to switch to a different station or play tapes or CDs that calm you and reinforce the new thought patterns you're trying to establish.

If the sight of an "Adult Bookstore" sign is a trigger for x-rated images, then change your routes to avoid them or learn to deliberately avert your eyes from seeing them. Believe me, I know some of this will sound foolish and insignificant but if you will continue in these practices, they will become habits and eventually automatic reflexes.

At that point you will begin to have dominance over these snares but never let down your defenses, because the enemy is not going to stop trying to defeat you by drawing you back into your addiction. Remember that you are an addict and the surest way to prevent or insure against a 'backslide' is to avoid getting into situations that subject you to highly sexually charged environments.

If you have friends or acquaintances who blatantly profess to engage in pornography or hedonistic, sexually immoral lifestyles, you will need to reduce your interaction with them. If you find that they are capable of influencing your thoughts in a negative way, those relationships are unhealthy for you. Ultimately, you'll discover that the most powerful and influential association you'll ever have is with yourself. You spend more time with yourself and your innermost thoughts than with anyone else and that's why it is so vitally important that you be very conscious and diligent to protect your own mind from destructive or de-edifying thoughts.

As you trace back to the roots of those thoughts which you've identified as triggers, begin to attach negative images or ideas to them as another method of diffusing them. For instance; if there is a certain woman whom you find fairly attractive who may suddenly begin making gestures implying that she's interested in you in a way that you know she ought not be, don't be blinded by the flattery of her attention. Here's a tip: no woman wakes up in the morning looking that good or that "together" like she does at the office everyday. If you must put your little imagination to work, try to imagine her with no makeup; a ratty-looking bath robe; rollers in her hair or tied up in a doo-rag; no under garments that defy the gravitational pull on certain body parts; corns and bunions on her feet, and bad morning breath. Again, I know this sounds silly but it works. You have to get creative using every weapon you can add to your arsenal to get an upper hand on this enemy. You meditate on that for a while and that woman won't be nearly as attractive to you. She'll even smell bad to you if you imagine her wearing a fragrance that repulses you. Your mind will see what your imagination convinces it that it sees.

I can remember one of the first practices I used when trying to gain control of my thoughts was the use of a simple command phrase, "Flesh be dead." This came from meditation of the writings of the Apostle Paul when he said [...I die daily] (I Corinthians 15:31) meaning that everyday he had to awaken his spirit man to dominate and squelch his fleshly desires by identifying with the death, burial and resurrection of Jesus Christ; putting asunder the old fleshly nature and arising into a new spiritual life which has the capacity to sustain a morally upright and decent manner of existence, free from domination by uncontrollable lusts and insatiable appetites.

Whenever I caught my mind drifting into such thoughts, I would say to myself, "flesh be dead – spirit man wake-up!" Immediately that impulse would subside because my thoughts would shift toward things associated with what I had spoken.

My Pastor has stated that one phrase he uses to keep his mind focused and diffuse certain wicked thoughts is simply, "I Love My Wife."

This was a profound confirmation for me because of two things: First, it let me know that even a man of impeccable honor and integrity such as he, has to fortify himself knowing that he is just as vulnerable to attack as anyone else; and secondly, that he uses practical and simplistic, non-spiritual techniques as well as spiritual principles of holiness and purity to combat both the natural and the spiritual aspects of sexual temptation.

I Corinthians 10:13 says, "There hath no temptation taken you but such as is common to man; but God is faithful, who will not suffer you to be tempted above that you are able; but will with the temptation make a way for you to escape, that ye may be able to bear it."

If you are truly repentant of your behavior and earnestly desire to be free of it forever, God will reveal to you what techniques will work specifically for you if those offered in this book are not enough. Just believe that He values you more than you value yourself and that if you seek Him for answers, He will never refuse His love and His wisdom.

As I bring this book to a close, I'm struck by the enormity of this subject. There are so many areas that can be affected by the disease of porn addiction that no one book could ever hope to address every aspect of it. I cannot help sometimes but to feel insignificant as a voice of alarm and admonishment in attempting to make an impact against such a pervasive societal illness. However,

I'm motivated by compassion and anger, two emotions I find totally essential as a driving force to push me forward into battle. I am angry about the years stolen from me due to blindness and deception and the altered state of mind in which I existed. I'm angry about the needless pain and insecurity I burdened my wife with during those years. I'm also angry about the fact that so many men, young and old are suffering tortured lives enslaved to secrecy and condemnation. I am at the same time moved with great compassion for these men because I know their turmoil. I've lived with their guilt, shame and fear. I've been spared the type of destruction and humiliation that many men have endured and surely many more will experience as casualties of this brutal war. I have also been blessed to discover the precious gift of Faith.

"Now Faith is the substance of things hoped for; the evidence of things not seen." (Hebrews 11:1) The beautiful thing about faith and being a believer is that we have a source of inspiration and hope that's always available to draw upon. Non-believers are limited to building their hopes only on what they can see and logically comprehend. If their outlook seems hopeless, circumstances will dictate that they respond as such. There are plenty of positive expressions and encouragement in the word of God.

The Bible is not a book of fictional bedtime stories or fables of what was. If you're just in need of more controversy or cynicism in your life you can always place emphasis on all the points of division between various religions or spiritual doctrines and 'debate' yourself into mental paralysis. However, if you will look at the Bible as a document of instruction and universal principles, you can override any oppression or source of negativity in your life by the meditation of an opposing ideology found in the scriptures. Our belief is that the Bible was written by man and inspired by a loving Father whose only desire is for you (His creation) to experience the best of life and a fulfilling and meaningful experience on earth.

As I stated from the beginning my intent in writing this book was to reach and relate to as many men as possible to share my experiences, some lessons learned and above all some hope and inspiration to help to strengthen your belief that pornography addiction can be beaten.

I now appeal specifically to those who may be non-believers and ask that you would please pay close attention to the following list of statements and read them through completely. I hope to drive home a point that I'll further explain at the end of these comments.

"The spirit indeed is willing, but the flesh is weak."

"Walk in the spirit and you will not fulfill the lust of the flesh."

"My son, forget not my teaching, but let your heart keep my commandments; for length of days and years of a life worth living, and tranquility shall they add to you."

"The righteous man walks in his integrity; his children are blessed after him."

"The lips of a loose woman drip honey as from a honeycomb and her mouth is as smooth as oil, but in the end she is as bitter as wormwood and sharp as a two edged sword. Her feet go down to death; her steps take hold on hell."

"He who walks uprightly walks securely, but he who takes a crooked way will be found out and punished."

"The earnings of the righteous lead to life; but the profits of the wicked lead to further sin."

"The thing a wicked man fears shall come upon him."

"For the righteous man may fall seven times and rise again, but the wicked shall fall by calamity."

"It is like a sport to a (self-confident) fool to do wickedness."

"The integrity of the upright shall guide them, but the perverseness of evil doers shall destroy them."

All of the previous statements were either paraphrased or directly quoted from the Bible. (*See* references on page 110). The point I hoped to emphasize to you is this; these few principles and words of instruction were written many hundreds if not thousands of years prior to our current state of human condition. Yet they are incredibly timeless pearls of wisdom that can be applied not just to the malady of porn addiction, but to the entire realm of humanity, which has battled against such sins of the flesh since the beginning of the recorded history of our existence.

This to me belies an understanding of the nature of man that could only have come from a divine, supreme Creator. An entity possessing the omniscience to have assigned to each of us a unique identity, design and purpose.

A being that intimately knows the complexities of our inner-workings and just what mis-steps or malfunctions would lead to our own self-destruction.

This is probably the strongest evidence ever impressed upon me that serves to bolster my faith in the God of the Bible and the undisputable truths found in His Word. No more precise and detailed instruction manual has ever been written for any man made product or creation, than this book which was lovingly written to guide us through the sometimes unbearably dark passageways of life.

You certainly do not require a belief in the God of the Bible or Jesus Christ to live a relatively normal existence and pass through life like so many others, on your way toward death and whatever future you have come to believe will be in store after your expiration. It's my belief that you will never experience the true freedom from pornography or any other such dysfunction that comes from the empowerment of your inner-man, which can only be acquired through a spiritual connection to the source of all truth, wisdom, understanding, honor, integrity and sacrificial Love, who is Almighty God.

For anyone who desires this connection and spiritual empowerment I invite you now to recite this simple prayer to follow. Speak it out loud and believe with all your heart that the Lord God above will receive your sincere prayer and in His undying mercy, welcome you into His kingdom of eternal life.

PRAYER OF SALVATION

Dear Lord, I come to you now just as I am. I know that I have not lived according to your will. I now confess Jesus Christ as my saviour and I believe by faith that He has cleansed me of my sin through the shedding of His blood. I believe that He died for me and that He rose from the grave, conquering death and bestowing upon me the gift of eternal life. I ask you Jesus, to come into my heart, and live in me and through me forevermore.

I thank you Lord for saving me today. In the name of Jesus I pray, Amen.

Whether you prayed the prayer above or chose not to at this time in your life, I would still love to hear from you and offer prayer, encouragement, friendly advice or just to be a compassionate listening ear if you so need.

If you did pray the prayer of salvation, I would recommend that you find a good Word teaching church in your local area where the power of God's principles are being taught and where lives are being changed for the better. Faith comes by hearing, and hearing the Word of God regularly and consistently.

Please correspond through email at:
www.u_b_restored_2@yahoo.com

SCRIPTURE REFERENCES

"The spirit indeed is willing, but the flesh is weak." (Matthew 26:41)

"Walk in the spirit and you will not fulfill the lust of the flesh." (Galatians 5:16) [paraphrase]

"My son, forget not my teaching, but let your heart keep my commandments; for length of days and years of a life worth living, and tranquility shall they add to you." (Proverbs 3:1-2 Amp.) [paraphrase]

"The righteous man walks in his integrity; his children are blessed after him." (Proverbs 20:7 Amp.)

"The lips of a loose woman drip honey as from a honeycomb and her mouth is as smooth as oil, but in the end she is as bitter as wormwood and sharp as a two edged sword. Her feet go down to death; her steps take hold on hell." (Proverbs 5:3-5 Amp.) [paraphrase]

"He who walks uprightly walks securely, but he who takes a crooked way will be found out and punished." (Proverbs 10:9 Amp.)

"The earnings of the righteous lead to life; but the profits of the wicked lead to further sin." (Proverbs 10:16 Amp.)

"The thing a wicked man fears shall come upon him." (Proverbs 10:24 Amp.) [paraphrase]

"For the righteous man may fall seven times and rise again, but the wicked shall fall by calamity." (Proverbs 24:16 Amp.)

"It is like a sport to a (self-confident) fool to do wickedness." (Proverbs 10:23 Amp.) [paraphrase]

"The integrity of the upright shall guide them, but the perverseness of evil doers shall destroy them." (Proverbs 11:3) [paraphrase]

Biography

Zerek L. Baker Sr. is a professional vocalist, lyricist and vocal arranger who has been involved in the music field for more than 30 years. He is now an active praise and worship leader using his musical gifts to lift up the name of the Lord in song and to minister to thousands on a regular basis.

As his occupation, Zerek currently works in Recorded Media Duplication and Technology for one of the largest ministries in the Chicagoland area. As a first-time author, he has taken on the challenge of addressing one of society's most taboo subjects after realizing that the process of his deliverance from this addiction may be helpful to someone else battling the same issues.

He and his wife Patrice have been married for 24 years and have two children attending college. They reside in the suburbs of Chicago, Illinois.

www.ingramcontent.com/pod-product-compliance
Lightning Source LLC
Chambersburg PA
CBHW051453290426
44109CB00016B/1733